What's Your Story?

A Beginner's Guide to Creating Effective Presentations *with* PowerPoint 2007

KAI CHUANG

I0006611

Published by PoPo Press (Phantomworks LLC)

Boston, MA

popopress@gmail.com

What's Your Story: A Beginner's Guide to Creating Effective Presentations with PowerPoint 2007. Copyright 2007 by Kai Chuang. All rights reserved. No part of this book may be reproduced or transmitted in any form or by any means, electronic or mechanical, including photocopying, recording, or by any information storage and retrieval system, without written permission from the publisher.

ISBN 978-0-6151-5806-8

Dedicated to Ru-Da Fan, my grandfather, who read to me when I was a child.

July 2007

Acknowledgments

I would like to acknowledge and thank the many people whose valuable contributions of time and energy made this work possible. In particular, I wish to express my gratitude to Neal Hartman, I-San Fan, Kathleen Poe, and Lindsey Chao for their help.

Table of Contents

Introduction

According to the Wall Street Journal, there are some 30 million PowerPoint presentations given every day around the world.[1] Although many argue - perhaps correctly - PowerPoint is a flawed tool that dumbs down communication, it has nevertheless become a de facto standard in just about every walk of life.   Furthermore, as PowerPoint gains ever-greater acceptance, its role has also expanded. No longer is PowerPoint used only for formal presentations. Now, book reports, memos, and even comic strips have been put in PowerPoint as it has become its own medium. In fact, at the time of this writing, there

---

[1] Sandberg, Jared. "Tips for PowerPoint: Go Easy on the Text Please, Spare Us." *Wall Street Journal*, 14 November 2006: B1.

is a social networking web site devoted to this new medium.[2] In my own experience, PowerPoint has become the most common way to communicate in corporations besides email and instant messaging.

That's all fine and good, except quantity doesn't necessarily mean quality. Suffice it to say, many PowerPoint presentations are bad. Some are very bad. We've all seen them, and maybe even were responsible for some of them. Ironically, one culprit of bad PowerPoint presentations is its ease of use because people can create them without having to give much thought. Consequently, PowerPoint becomes an excuse for not developing a well-structured and polished communications plan. It's too bad, because PowerPoint can be a tremendously useful tool.

The problem stems from the fact that despite how much PowerPoint is used in businesses, schools, and many other situations, we've never been trained on how to use this tool properly. Closing this skills gap is harder than it might otherwise appear because creating an effective and professional PowerPoint presentation requires a set of *interdisciplinary* skills, not just being a software jockey. It's necessary to know a little about communications techniques, information design principles, and presentation skills. While many books teach how to use PowerPoint the software, and many more cover the other subject matters, these books don't combine all the ingredients in a

---

[2] SlideShare. 13 February 2007 <http://www.slideshare.net>.

manner that's easy for beginners to learn. That's what I hope to address.

Who this book is for

This book's target audience is students and professionals who know their way around PowerPoint (or similar software), but have not had extensive experience in creating professional presentations. Rather than discovering what works through trial and error, you should be able to accelerate improvements in your presentation skills by practicing the techniques described in the following chapters. Although this book's goal is not to turn you into a master practitioner, it is to provide you a set of basic tools for building a solid foundation and instilling the confidence to create effective presentations.

What's in this book

We begin with an overview of the ingredients commonly found in effective presentations. Next, a select number of PowerPoint 2007 features that can be used to synthesize these ingredients are discussed. Then, a simple step-by-step cookbook approach illustrates how to develop and combine these ingredients to create effective presentations. Finally, our cookbook methods are put in practice in an example about a fictitious company.

A number of general design principles and other rules of thumb are cited throughout the book. In order to achieve our stated objectives - giving beginners a set of practical tools, some spontaneity in the creative process is sacrificed for structure. It is hoped that with a solid - even if formulaic - foundation, readers can later inject creativity and individual styles into their PowerPoint presentations.

What's not in this book

This book does not contain detailed how-to tutorials of using the PowerPoint 2007 software, nor does it teach advanced techniques to experienced practitioners.

What if you don't have PowerPoint 2007

Don't worry. Although a number of techniques are illustrated using features in PowerPoint 2007, the concepts do transfer well to older versions such as PowerPoint 2003 as well as to other presentation software packages such as Keynote for the Mac and Adobe Flash.

Note on notational convention

As the term *PowerPoint* has become a part of our cultural vocabulary, in order to avoid confusion over referring to the software application, the electronic documents produced, and the physical act of communicating, unless otherwise noted, "PowerPoint 2007" will refer to the software application, and "presentation" will refer to the corresponding document or an exhibition in front of an audience, depending on context.

Ingredients of an Effective Presentation

For some, creating a PowerPoint presentation can be a daunting task, whereby so much effort is spent on producing the electronic document that the presentation becomes an end in itself, rather than a means to an end. For others, PowerPoint is used as a crutch for poor presentation skills, whereby the presenter simply reads what's written on the slides in front of an audience.

PowerPoint 2007 - or any other software - is but a tool that can enhance your telling a compelling story, which, at the end of the day, is the whole point.

For these reasons, we take a holistic approach to the creative process, and begin by reviewing ingredients found in winning presentations.

Clear purpose

What do you hope to accomplish with your presentation? Do you want to inform, educate, or to persuade? A presentation with a clear purpose comes across as a deliberate conversation rather than a rambling of disjointed ideas. Having a clear purpose not only provides focus for the creative process, but has practical implications as well. In particular, the structure of your presentation will likely depend on the specific goals you hope to achieve.

Tailored to the audience

How familiar is your audience with the subject matter of your presentation? Are you presenting to a sympathetic or tough crowd, or perhaps a mixture of both? Although you might not want survey everyone to answer to these questions, you can do some simple things - like finding out who will be in your audience and their roles - to get a feel for the answers. Knowing a little something about your audience and its needs goes a long way towards accomplishing the purpose of your presentation. A great presentation tailored to the audience's level of knowledge and topics of interest will engage the audience and proactively address your audience's opinions and potential biases about the subject matter.

A compelling story

Your "story" is the heart of your presentation. The word "story" hopefully conjures up memories of listening to a fantastic tale by the fireside or reading a captivating yarn that you couldn't put down. A great story can evoke the senses, inspire the imagination, and compel action. Like a great story, an effective presentation can tap into rational reasoning as well as deep-rooted emotions to compel an audience to think, feel, and act. Perhaps unlike a real "story", however, an effective presentation keeps its story line to only what is essential to accomplish its purpose. In other words, the "story" has to be tight.

The "story" metaphor should not be taken literally, however. It's not necessary to construct a presentation like some Hollywood script (unless you are really pitching one to Steven Spielberg). In fact, actually telling a story in most academic and business situations will likely come across as unprofessional.

Developed for the right medium

Will your presentation be projected on a screen in front of a live audience, displayed on individual computers during a conference call, or emailed as a standalone document (i.e. read without narrative)? As you can imagine, a presentation projected on a screen might have to abide by stricter limits on font size and color than one used as a standalone document to ensure readability. Conversely, a presentation consumed in a standalone fashion requires greater detail because there is no presenter to explain everything. Therefore, it's necessary to know upfront how your presentation will be used since its structure and content can vary depending on the delivery format. An effective presentation is customized for the target delivery format and looks great in that format.

A great performance

Can you think of a movie or theatrical performance that had a terrific story line, but the acting was so bad that it ruined your experience? A live presentation is like a movie or theatrical performance in that the telling of the story is as important as the story itself. A great presenter is like a great actor in that she makes the story believable and come alive. In this sense, a presentation is an experienced product that doesn't end with an electronic document, but with a great performance. Quite simply, substance alone is not enough. Style counts!

Getting the Most Out of PowerPoint 2007

PowerPoint 2007 is a part of the Office 2007 suite, and contains many new features wrapped inside a brand new user interface. Gone are the familiar file menus, replaced by the Ribbon with tabs. The Ribbon seems more intuitive, but does takes a little getting used to, especially for users accustomed to previous versions when trying to find familiar commands in new locations.

Although there are many new features in PowerPoint 2007, our attention will focus on functionalities that are most useful for our purposes. This means some of the features we will be working with are not new in PowerPoint 2007, and is good news to people already familiar with previous versions of PowerPoint. In fact, it's possible to apply all the concepts in the following chapters using PowerPoint 2003 (for example) as most of the PowerPoint 2007 features we consider have some work-around - such as importing graphics in lieu of creating them in SmartArt.

Themes, Layouts, & Quick Styles

Some of the best things about PowerPoint 2007, especially for beginners, are its upgraded themes, layouts, and quick styles features. Themes are sets of prebuilt templates, 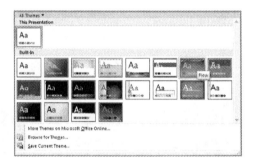 each implementing a consistent look and feel so you don't have to worry about creating that consistency from scratch. As we'll see, achieving consistency is actually pretty important. What themes do for the look and feel of a presentation, layouts do the same for the organization of content on each slide by providing pre-configured patterns based on content type. Although layouts is not a new feature in PowerPoint 2007, it is more prominently displayed and easier to access. Quick Styles allows you to tryout different themes, colors, and many other attributes on-the-fly without having to apply changes first. This feature is particularly useful when you're not sure what "looks best" and would like to quickly test a number of different looks.

SmartArt

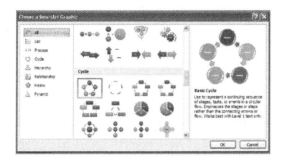

If you've ever had to create chevrons - or any other conceptual diagrams - from scratch, you probably will appreciate PowerPoint 2007's new SmartArt feature. SmartArt is a collection of commonly used diagrams with an easy way to insert text into the diagrams. Say you want a cycle diagram like the one pictured above. No problem. You can simply choose among the many cycle diagrams from SmartArt and easily modify the number of elements in the cycle or attach text to them.

Slide Master

If you don't like any of the built-in themes, you can modify one or create your own by using the Slide Master feature. Slide Master lets you define attributes such as font family, font size and color, bullet styles, and

location of header and footer for an entire presentation. This is particularly useful because otherwise you would have to make these changes on every slide.

Charts

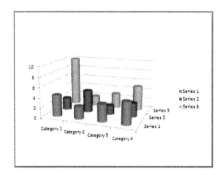

Although PowerPoint 2007 provides some very good charting capabilities, we favor creating charts in Excel in this book. For reasons to be discussed later, it's often better to create charts in Excel and paste them as images in your presentation. Excel charts are sufficient for most situations you are likely to encounter, unless you have special needs such as presenting complex scientific data.

Presenter View

When using two displays, presenter view provides the ability to show different content on each display. This feature comes in particularly handy for showing the speaker's notes on the presenter's monitor while projecting the presentation on another display. Additionally, presenter view also allows the presenter to preview what the next click will add to the screen, such as a new bullet in a list or a new slide.

Animations & Transitions

The animations feature lets you script the sequence of events on each slide by associating actions (e.g. to appear) with objects (e.g. a graphic). Additionally, each action can be triggered based on a mouse-click, a timer, or a change in status from another event. Slide transitions are special effects used when a new slide is introduced during a slideshow.

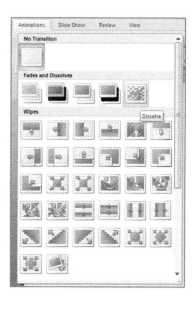

When used effectively, animations and slide transitions can greatly enhance the audience experience.

AutoShapes

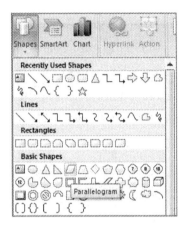

If you can't find what you're looking for in SmartArt, then AutoShapes could be for you. Short of creating custom images using another software program, AutoShapes provides the ability to create custom diagrams using basic building blocks such as rectangles, ovals, and cylinders.

STEP 1 Define Topic & Goals

Choosing a presentation topic is usually pretty straightforward. Sometimes, a topic is already chosen for you (e.g. give a summary of your research project). What is often more difficult but equally important, however, is limiting the scope of your subject matter to only what is necessary to tell your story. As a practical matter, the narrower you can make your topic, the better. Even if you're planning to present on a vast subject such as global warming, it's likely you would be focused on only a tiny fraction such as the effects of methane gas from the melting of permafrost in Siberia.

Before you begin working on a presentation, ask yourself what you hope and expect to accomplish? For example, do you wish to raise the audience's awareness about subject, persuade them to take a course of action, or sell them a product? Depending on your answer, your presentation would likely vary not only in its content, but also in its level of complexity and the amount of effort required. As such, figuring out the end game is crucial before you start making slides.

With that in mind, the following table illustrates some common uses of presentations:

Presentation scenario	Intended outcome	Example
Inform	Increase awareness	Status report
Educate	Teach skills	Software training
Persuade	Influence opinion	Project summary
Sell	Make a sale	Sales pitch

As outlined above, each presentation scenario addresses a distinct set of needs, and should be approached differently. By considering subject matter together with intended outcome, you're off to a great start in creating effective presentations.

In general, crafting a presentation to inform is easier than creating one to sell because making a sale requires a deeper understanding of the audience's psychological needs, potential objections, and how to overcome them. Whereas your supervisor might just be happy hearing about the latest developments on your research project, your customer will be more skeptical of your sales pitch, especially if you're selling something expensive (like a multi-million dollar software package). Of course, not all situations fit nicely into one of these categories. Sometimes, a hybrid presentation is needed - maybe in order to make a sale you have to first educate the customer about the problem that your product would solve. Nevertheless, this simplified view sheds some light on how to approach developing presentations for different situations.

As we consider how to meet the psychological needs of our audience, we can benefit from recognizing this is a general issue of how to influence others. There's actually a lot of research studying influence that is quite useful to us. Some of the most practical results in this field come from Robert Cialdini's work.

In what's commonly referred to Cialdini's Six Weapons of Influence,[3] six principles play key roles in the art of persuasion:

Liking

People are more likely to say "yes" to people they like. In the context of making a presentation, it helps to develop a personal connection with the audience such as knowing something about them or identifying real similarities. If you don't know your audience on a personal level, take some time to make informal introductions at the beginning of your presentation meeting.

Reciprocity

People repay in kind. Quite simply, people in general will be nice to you if you are nice to them. When making a presentation, be respectful of the audience's questions and comments by handling them gracefully. Also, be respectful of other people's time by being prepared and delivering a well-rehearsed presentation.

---

[3] Cialdini, Robert B. (October 2001). "Harnessing the Science of Persuasion". *Harvard Business Review*, 72-79.

Social proof

People are more likely to go along if they know others have already done so. For example, if you want to recommend a new course of action, your suggestions will more likely be accepted if you can show that other people have already signed-on to your proposal. Therefore, mentioning with whom you've worked on your proposal and who else is on-board is a great way to establish social proof.

Consistency

People want to stick to their commitments, particularly those made voluntarily in public. This is why PowerPoint presentations are sometimes used not to introduce new information, but to confirm agreement on what's already been discussed with audience members in advance. So, if you're recommending a course of action, see if you can get your audience's agreement on key issues before the presentation.

Authority

People tend to defer to authority figures or experts. This means you want to establish credibility early in your presentation, especially if the audience is unfamiliar with your background on the subject matter. But be careful, you don't want to come across as being arrogant either. One way to establish credibility tactfully for a project status presentation is describing any relevant experience you possess as well as with whom you've worked.

Scarcity

People want what they can't have, or are about to lose. In fact, research has shown that people are more afraid of losing than gaining something of the exact same value. There are some useful results from these findings. For example, in a sales presentation for power-efficient computers, you want to highlight unique features and benefits of your product over the competition's or the status quo. Additionally, instead of framing benefits in terms of how much money can be saved from lower utilities bills, you should describe the benefits in terms of stopping wasting money on electricity expenses.

It goes without saying that the principles above are meant to help you create more effective presentations by providing insights to aspects of human behavior, and are not meant to be used as tricks on an unsuspecting audience. In practice, sophisticated audience members can usually see through attempts at manipulation anyway, so it's best to exercise good judgment and apply these principles in an ethical manner.

STEP 2 Determine Delivery Format & Time Available

Delivery format refers to how your presentation will be used, or consumed, by your audience. There are a number of common delivery formats you might encounter in typical academic and business settings. In particular:

• Live delivery: presentation is projected on a screen in front of an audience and accompanied by a presenter's narrative.

• Conference call or other virtual delivery method: presentation is viewed by an audience on individual computer screens or in hardcopies, and accompanied by a presenter's narrative. Increasingly, video conference is also used as a virtual delivery method.

• Standalone delivery: presentation is consumed by an audience in whatever way the audience chooses with no accompanying narrative.

Knowing how your presentation will be consumed is important because delivery format presents practical constraints on content design. For example, if your presentation will be projected on a screen in a 40-person conference room, you want to use a font size so that persons sitting in the back can still read the text on your slides. You want to avoid making a presentation with people squinting because they will either be focusing their attention on trying to see, or be tuning out completely.

To a large extent, the minimum font size for a live delivery depends on the distance between your audience and the viewing screen as well as the size of the screen. Although it's possible to calculate this number, the easiest way to determine font size is to just run some tests in the conference room by projecting a blank slide with different sized text and see which looks best (Don't laugh. If it's an important presentation and you have access to the room you should absolutely do this). If checking out the facilities ahead of time is not possible, you should be safe in using a font size no smaller than 24 pts.

Although font size is less of a concern in virtual or standalone delivery settings, there are other issues. For instance, it's a lot harder to engage audience members and focus their attention in a virtual delivery environment because they could be multitasking on other activities. We will return to this issue in a later chapter about rehearsing for a presentation. Even trickier is the standalone delivery because you can't explain anything in person, so your presentation has to speak for itself. As a result, more details would be needed to ensure there is sufficient information to communicated your ideas and prevent them from being taken out of context. Fortunately, pure standalone presentations are rare in practice for these reasons (better medium would be a memo or paper), but you should be aware of the unique challenges in case you have to create one.

Of course, you can't always know exactly how your presentation will be used, but you can anticipate some likely scenarios and plan accordingly. Perhaps hardcopies from a sales presentation to a customer in the marketing department are forwarded to someone in finance for review. Because your presentation was tailored to marketing's concerns, it would probably not have a favorable review from the finance department's perspective. You could avoid this sort of scenario by not providing any hardcopies or arranging for a follow-up conversation with the finance department to review the presentation together.

Time management is often overlooked when creating presentations, but is actually very important because the amount of time available - both actual working time and total elapsed time - limits what can reasonably be done with a presentation. Furthermore, because the creative process is iterative, total elapsed time is as important as the actual working time. All else being equal, a presentation developed over a period of time will be better than one done in a single sitting. So, start early if possible.

Time available also affects the amount of media and interactivity that can be developed for the presentation. Many people like to make use of pretty graphics and fancy transitions, but progressively richer media take more time to develop. Generally speaking, if you're limited on time you should target a lower fidelity presentation. To give you an idea for how much time is involved, see below for a breakout that's typical of a presentation with one hour run time:

Available working time	Total elapsed time	Target fidelity
4 hours or less	1 day or less	Text
4 to 10 hours	A few days	Text, data charts, simple graphics

Available working time	Total elapsed time	Target fidelity
10 to 20 hours	1 to 2 weeks	Text, data charts, graphics, animation, transitions

Finally, you should determine how long the presentation needs to be. If you're making a live presentation, this is usually measured in terms of time (e.g. one hour meeting). Although presentations created for different situations would likely contain dissimilar content, there are similarities when it comes to the number of slides that can be presented for a given period of time. In particular, a 3-5 minutes/slide on average, not including title and other transition slides, is a good pace. For example, a one-hour presentation might breakdown into the following:

Activity	Duration
Audience settling in	~ 5 min
Presentation	10-15 content slides @ 3-5 min/slide ~ 50 min

Activity	Duration
Q&A	~ 5-10 min
Total	60 min

STEP 3 Assess Audience Needs

Your presentation is not all about you. It is about your audience, too. It's not enough to just have a great story. That great story must also be relevant. For your presentation to be relevant, you need to know a little something about your audience. For a typical presentation, you want to find out:

- Audience's level of background about your subject.
- Any special interests or particular biases.
- Whether audience is sympathetic or hostile.

Luckily, you probably won't have to address the entire spectrum of needs for everyone in the audience. There will be only a subset of people whom you have to really target. These are the individuals you are trying to inform, educate, persuade, or whatever. In a school setting, if you're giving a presentation to the class, you would obviously want to ensure the professor's needs are addressed. But it probably would be okay if you can't address all the students' needs. If the makeup of your audience is complicated, it might be a good idea to segment people into different stakeholder groups and their respective needs. This analysis is especially helpful when there is a mixed audience with different levels of background knowledge and needs, and allows tailoring of content most effectively. Although this task might seem complicated and sounds like a lot of work, the good news is that in most cases, this is a simple exercise because an approximation is usually good enough. For instance, in a business setting you could segment people by their job functions and responsibilities. In doing so, you would be able to evaluate who can make decisions, who can only influence the decision making process, and who are just along for the ride. Even if you're not 100% correct, it would still be a lot better than having no clue at all.

Once key members of your audience are identified, gauging their knowledge on the subject matter allows you to include just the right amount of background material, because repeating things people already know will surely lose them a few minutes into your presentation. Similarly, talking over people's heads will lose them too. It gets more complicated. If your audience is comprised of people with different levels of knowledge, it can be even more challenging to create content that works for everybody. In a business environment, this situation happens more frequently than you might think. For example, you might have to give a sales presentation pitching your company's latest product to a customer. In this scenario, you have to first make a pitch to the business buyer - who wants to hear about why your product is going to help increase revenue, reduce costs, etc. Then, you might have to give a different pitch to the customer's IT department - who wants to know how your product will integrate with their systems. The business buyer might not care about how your product implements Voice Over IP, and the IT buyer might not care about the Return On Investment. Not only do the two audiences have different knowledge about your subject, they care about different things entirely. You might be better off having two different presentations (but portions of the presentations can and will likely contain the same material).

As illustrated above, it's important to be aware of what the audience cares about pertaining to your subject matter. To the extent possible you want to proactively address these interests or concerns in your presentation, or they could manifest on their own in undesirable ways, such as irrelevant questions. Ideally, you would have an opportunity to get a feel for what's on the audience's mind so content can be tailored accordingly. Often, all you have to do is to ask. In practice, asking is easy to do because people in general would appreciate your taking an interest in their concerns. Not only will you find out a bunch of things needed for your presentation, but you also get a chance to build goodwill.

Sometimes, you won't know for sure exactly what your audience needs, or might not have an easy way to find out. Fortunately, there are ways to get a good enough estimate. For example, it's possible to get a sense of an audience's interests based on presentation type. If you're making presentation to report project status, expect people will want to hear about key accomplishments, issues, milestones, and next steps. You could also estimate based on the audience members' roles or job functions in an organization. For instance, it goes without saying if you're making a presentation to colleagues in the marketing department about a launching new product, your audience will likely want to hear about market sizing and segmentation.

Finally, depending on your subject matter and your relationship with the audience, you might also have to demonstrate enough credibility to be making the claims you're making. If you find yourself in this situation, it's better to establish credibility early on to avoid lingering doubts throughout your presentation. There are a number of ways to establish credibility, ranging from describing the methodology that was followed in a research project to naming the people you worked with to arrive at your conclusions.

STEP 4 Outline & Storyboard

By focusing on your goals and paying attention to the needs of the audience, your presentation should embody a well-crafted plot. This means the content should be carefully developed such that each part contributes deliberately to the larger story. Managing content to only what is necessary to make your case is particularly important because you want to lead your audience through a well-thought-out line of reasoning; extraneous information can not only decrease your arguments' effectiveness, but actually confuse the audience. But how do you actually go about crafting a plot? By the end of *STEP 3 Assess Audience Needs*, you have already developed a good feel for what you want to convey. Well, creating an outline is a great way to organize these ideas into a plot.

Your outline not only sets the length of your presentation, but also determines the types of content that should reside in different parts of the presentation. Consequently, you want to get the outline right before starting on storyboarding or authoring since it can be a big deal to change it later as content and supporting media would all have to change.

Creating an outline using PowerPoint 2007

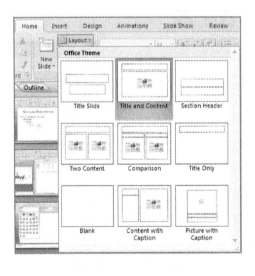

The easiest way to create an outline is to build it right in PowerPoint 2007 by starting a new document and simply insert slides, one for each topic in your outline. Go ahead and insert a bunch of new Title and Content slides from the ribbon - you can delete what you don't need later. The reason we choose Title and Content is because it provides a generic layout that can be easily changed later during storyboarding. Additionally, Title and Content furnishes the Title area needed for your outline. Incidentally,

42

because the Title area is likely the first - and sometimes only - thing your audience will notice, you want to make sure content in the Title area is exactly right.

Once you have bunch of new slides, create your outline by simply typing a headline in the *Title* area of each slide. You can use the *Normal View* in PowerPoint 2007 to quickly review and edit the headlines that

comprise your outline. As mentioned above, since headlines could be the only thing your audience will read, make sure they are worded deliberately. In general, each headline should communicate the essence of that slide in a succinct manner, and for good reasons. First, a succinct headline is likely to the point and cogent; second, a succinct headline is shorter and can better fit in the *Title* area, ideally on a single line (two lines are okay as we'll see in an example later). Additionally, headlines should be written in active voices - not as passive phrases - if in so doing can communicate more powerfully. Having said that, not every headline has to be in an active voice, nor do all headlines have to be complete sentences. The following table provides some examples of active versus passive headlines:

43

Passive headline	Active headline
Recommendation	We need to change course
Scope of investigation	Focused on 1st order effects
Features & benefits	Feature-rich yet simple to use

As you continue writing headlines, they should begin to read like the outline to your story. Although there are many ways to craft an outline or to tell a story, it's instructive to look at common presentation scenarios and corresponding outline templates that can be used as a starting point (note: the templates are written generically. Update them as appropriate for your situation).

Status

A Status presentation can be used to provide updates on something you've been working on. In such a presentation, you are usually informing peers, supervisors, or other stakeholders who are already familiar with the subject matter.

1. Introduction (background)

2. Scope of work or project
3. Key findings and accomplishments to date
4. Major issues for attention
5. Progress against schedule & budget
6. Areas for further study (next steps)
7. Q&A

Training

A Training presentation is commonly used by instructors as a way to guide classroom learning. Furthermore, many Flash and other web-based training are created first as PowerPoint presentations and then converted to their respective formats. Although professional training presentations used by instructors incorporate not only general presentation principles, but also instructional design theories, the ease of use and availability of PowerPoint means many non-training professionals will probably create a training presentation at some point.

1. Introduction
2. Lesson objectives
3. Topic 1
4. …
5. Topic n
6. Summary

Project Summary

A Project Summary presentation is commonly used to communicate key outcomes of a study and to influence your audience to adopt resultant recommendations. This type of presentation differs from the status presentation in that you are less concerned about reporting progress, and more interested in affecting opinions. A project summary presentation often has to articulate what is the issue, why it's important, why anything needs to be done at all, and why your recommendations are the right ones.

1. Introduction
2. Problem statement or background
3. Project overview
4. Methodology (approach)
5. Key findings
6. Recommendations
7. Implementation plan
8. Next steps
9. Q&A

Sales

A Sales presentation is used to pitch a product or service to a prospective customer audience, and usually takes place after a professional relationship has already been established with a member of the customer's organization. Frequently, an initial generic sales presentation is delivered to a group of stakeholders with various job responsibilities and interests. Depending on what you're selling, it might be necessary to follow-up with certain stakeholders with more targeted sales presentations tailored to their needs. As such, sales presentations can vary quite a bit. Nevertheless, their objectives are often the same, since your goal is not to just inform or persuade someone, as challenging a task as that could be. Rather, it's all that and more, because you're trying to get people to make a purchase decision. This is where *STEP 3 Assess Audience Needs*, becomes even more important. Suffice it to say, there is an art to making successful sales pitches, so we won't attempt to cover everything here. However, what we can say about creating good sales presentations is that you have to quickly get to the point and clearly articulate a compelling value proposition, in addition to anticipating likely objections and addressing them proactively.

1. Introduction
2. Your understanding of their needs or problem
3. Quantified impact of their problem
4. How your product/service addresses their problem
5. Key features and benefits
6. How will it work for the customer
7. Costs and estimated return on investment
8. Customer testimonials
9. Proposed next steps (towards closing the deal)

10. Q&A

Once you have a completed outline, test it by reading the headlines from beginning to end. Do they tell the story you want to convey? Is it a compelling story? Iterate and keep making adjustments until you are satisfied.

When you are satisfied with your outline, you are ready to proceed to the next step, storyboarding. Originated at the Walt Disney Studio, storyboarding was used as a means to quickly mock-up animated scenes before artists start drawing. This practice has since been adopted for numerous other applications in designing animations, movies, online training, user interfaces, and is a great tool for creating presentations. For our purposes, storyboarding involves taking your outline and determining the content and their layout for each slide.

Depending on the complexity of your presentation, whether you're planning to review in-progress work with others, and personal preference, storyboarding can range from just thinking through what you want on each slide and updating the slide layouts, to actually making mock-ups of each slide (on paper or in PowerPoint 2007). For our purposes, we will use the former technique because it's easy to make changes in layout by selecting a new one from the available templates that works with the planned content for a slide. Even if you don't see a layout you like, it's simple to create a new template.

STEP 5 Author Content & Refine

By now, you should have a pretty good idea what your presentation is going to look like. The next step, then, is to populate the outline and storyboard created in *STEP 4 Outline & Storyboard* with content. Just as you were deliberate in crafting the outline and storyboard, you want to be as deliberate in designing each slide to achieve the intended effect.

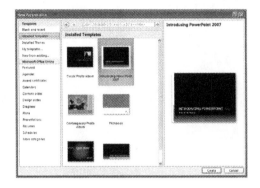

Let's begin by giving your presentation an overall look and feel. It's pretty simple to do this in PowerPoint 2007 through the use of *Templates*. Each *Template* embodies a complete system of look and feel components such as slide design, font definition, and paragraph spacing that can be used to create a distinct and consistent style for your presentation. For those of you familiar with web design, *Templates* are conceptually similar to Cascading Style Sheets.

As you contemplate the overall look and feel for your presentation, it's a good time to consider some User Interface, or UI, design principles. These are a set of guidelines commonly used to design user-friendly software programs that facilitate efficient information exchange between people and computers, and address issues such as determining colors of the graphical user interface, setting spacing among text blocks, and enforcing alignment of objects on the screen. As you can see, we face many of the same issues when developing presentations. Therefore, it makes good sense to follow relevant UI principles in order to not only enhance the overall aesthetics of your presentation, but also improve its ability to communicate.

Although there are many UI design principles that apply to software, luckily we need to look at only a few.

Overall consistency

The overall look and feel of your presentation should be consistent (reason why we began by picking a template). This means the same font family, font size for different text types (e.g. headings, bullets and sub-bullets), and color scheme should be adopted throughout your presentation, unless you deliberately design otherwise. Similarly, content sizing should be consistent across slides. For example, if there are a number of slides, each with a data chart, the physical dimensions of the charts should be approximately equal. However, the charts don't have to be located at exactly the same spot on every slide. In fact, it would be better to pick a couple of locations for chart placement (e.g. left half and right half of a slide) and alternate between slides.[4]

Grouping & anchoring

People tend to visually perceive the environment around them by looking for patterns and structure. Even when taking a Rorschach test we try to interpret seemingly random ink blots in terms of something they resemble. This observation has important implications on presentation design because

---

[4] Tufte, Edward R. *Envisioning Information*. Cheshire: Graphics Press LLC, 1990. 83.

presentations usually have to communicate a lot of information in an efficient manner. Our challenge is made more difficult because audience members might not be paying attention or could be sitting very far away. For these reasons, your presentation should be designed in a way that helps the audience to quickly zero in on the key messages and make sense of the information presented.

One way to facilitate this natural pattern recognition process is by grouping content on a slide into points of focus. Fortunately, there is a lot of research on visual perception and grouping. One such study resulted in the Gestalt Laws of Organization,[5] which embodies principles that describe how information is visually perceived, and can be quite helpful:

• Proximity: objects that are physically close together tend to be grouped together. For example, sub-bullets should be spaced closer to their parent bullet point than to the next bullet point.

• Similarity: objects that share common characteristics such as color, size, or shape tend to be grouped together. For example, icons can be used in conjunction with text to convey a new layer of information on top of an existing layer. Conversely, similarity characteristics can also be used to distinguish one object from another. When applied to bullet

---

[5] "Perception (psychology)," Microsoft® Encarta® Online Encyclopedia 2006 http://encarta.msn.com © 1997-2006 Microsoft Corporation. All Rights Reserved.

points, the similarity principle says a sub-bullet point should have a smaller font-size, font-weight, and different bullet style from its parent in order to visually cue the parent-child relationship.

- Simplicity: people perceive visually using the simplest and most stable of possible organizations. Therefore, graphics, animations, or SmartArt designs should be as simple as necessary.

By making use of these principles, you can smartly group content on each slide to aid visual perception. However, grouping alone is not enough because even groups of information can still take time to process. Hence, you want to also selectively highlight content on each slide so that they stand out. But are all content created equal?

Because our writing system produces text that's read from left to right and from top to bottom, an audience will process information on a slide in the same manner. Consequently, consistent with intuition, the most important ideas or results should be presented above secondary ones. Not coincidentally, this is another reason why the headline is so important because it's likely to be noticed first. Therefore, in addition to writing a great headline, it helps to have the headline clearly stand out. There are a couple of ways this can be done. One way is to visually separate your headline by either inserting a horizontal line beneath it or applying a different background color to the

Title area. This treatment also makes the headline appear "anchored" and not floating in space. Another way is to make a headline's font size larger than those of other text on the slide. In practice, headlines often are anchored and have larger font.

Colors

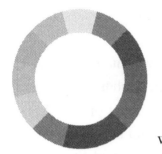 Colors can make a huge difference in both the information value and aesthetic appeal of a presentation. Although some people have a natural talent for choosing and mixing colors that just work, there are a few rules of thumb for the rest of us for using colors successfully:

• For a live presentation, use a dark color for the slide's background if in a room with light decor and a light background color if in a room with dark decor.

• Create a high contrast between the color of a slide's background and that of the text (e.g. black text on white background or yellow text on blue background).

• Don't go crazy on colors. Use colors to emphasize, not just because you can.

• If unsure about matching colors, choose colors that are opposite of each other in a color wheel (e.g. green and purple).

- Use of a primary color against a muted background can be especially effective in highlighting details or patterns.[6]

While colors can really spruce up our presentation, and may even be fun to work with, there are a couple of gotchas to keep in mind. In particular, when using colors to communicate information, choose colors that can be seen by people who are color-blind (red green color-blindness is most common). Additionally, choose colors that display well in grayscale in case your presentation is printed in hardcopy.

Whitespace & balance

Whitespace - empty space on a slide not occupied by content - performs an important function in visual perception and information processing by reducing clutter that in turn allows patterns to form. Although creating whitespace seems easy - just don't fill up a slide with content, there are some basic rules:

- Use at least double space for text paragraphs to improve readability.
- Spacing between bullet points should be greater than within the paragraph of a bullet point.

---

[6] Tufte, Edward R. *Envisioning Information*. Cheshire: Graphics Press LLC, 1990. 83.

- Reserve space around the edges of slides, and create space between different content objects (e.g. a chart with accompanying bullet points).

- If there is only a small amount of content, distribute them evenly on the slide; however, don't significantly increase font size just to take up space. Although PowerPoint 2007 can automatically size text, use this feature judiciously in order to preserve text size consistency throughout the presentation.

- If there is a lot of content on a slide, consider moving some to a new slide.

Although whitespace tends to distribute content evenly on a slide, the result could still appear unbalanced. Imagine this slide were printed out and suspended by a string attached to the center of the page, and each content object (e.g. text area, graphic) had mass proportional to its size and complexity. Would the paper tip to one side? If so, the slide's balance can probably be improved by moving certain content objects, modifying font size and weight of texts, or some combination.

Content guide

Even with a great setup to introduce your topic and a fine outline to tell your story, it can still be too easy for the audience to focus on individual slides and lose sight of the big picture. When this happens, some audience members might tune out completely while others try to figure out what's going on by raising irrelevant concerns, asking ill-timed questions, or wanting to spend more time on secondary issues. Therefore, it's important to help the audience incorporate additional information within an overall context. Fortunately, there are a number of simple techniques to address this issue:

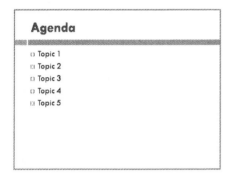

- Create an agenda slide and place it at the beginning of your presentation. An agenda slide provides a roadmap for the audience such that it's easier to integrate low-level details with high-level themes.

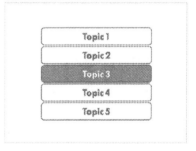

- Use segue slides to move among high-level themes. A segue slide provides a visual cue to shift focus to a new topic. There are two types of segue slides in common use. One type simply displays the next topic, while the other type highlights the next topic among the full list of topics.

- Tabs can be used to provide contextual information at all times by displaying the main topics as a series of tabs on every slide and highlighting the current topic. Although tabs can be

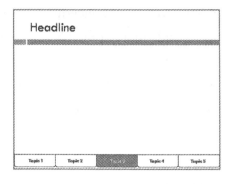

effective, there are some disadvantages including taking up space on every slide and limiting the number of topics that can be tabbed without appearing cluttered.

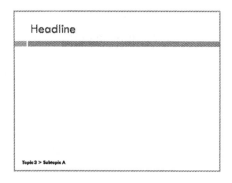

- Breadcrumbs, like tabs, provide contextual information by displaying the current topic relative to the main subject matter. Whereas tabs are used for linear topics, breadcrumbs can be used

for topics that have some hierarchical relationship.

Themes & templates

Fortunately, it's possible to achieve many of our UI design goals by using PowerPoint 2007's built-in Themes. However, some built-in Themes are rather colorful and might not be very effective at communicating information and could even appear inappropriate in a professional context. When choosing a Theme, then, simple styles with clean lines are preferred over those with fancy background pictures or cute 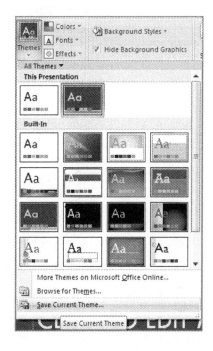 graphics. If you don't see a Theme that you like, you can create your own by customizing existing or designing new Slide Masters and Slide Layouts, and save them as a new Theme.

Text

Despite recent backlashes by pundits against using bullet points, they still form the foundation of most presentations out there today and are not likely to go away anytime soon. As such, bullet points do play an important role, and can be used effectively if some common-sense guidelines are observed:

- Arrange bullet points in order of importance.
- Have no more than three levels of bullet/sub-bullet points.
- Ensure parallel construction in words and phrases, clauses, and lists after a colon. For example, use active and passive voices consistently, and don't mix gerunds (e.g. walking) with infinitives (e.g. to walk) in a bullet point.[7]

Data visualization

Frequently, there will be a need to communicate data or ideas that can't be easily expressed through text alone. For example, you might want to show findings from an experiment or results from a customer survey. In such cases, the most natural way to convey the information would be via charts, tables, or diagrams. In fact, figuring out the best way to represent information of all types is an on-going challenge when working with presentations because screen real estate is limited and you usually want to use data to make some point. The main problem becomes distilling the essence from what could be massive amounts of data without introducing bias, while highlighting key outcomes so they are readily apparent. When done effectively, data visualization can be not only more efficient and effective than text for communicating information, but also more interesting to look at and better at keeping an audience's attention. Although there is definitely an element of artistic expression in creating good data

---

[7] "Parallel Structure." *The Owl at Purdue.* 2 March 2007.
<http://owl.english.purdue.edu/owl/resource/623/01/>.

visualization, there are also standard methods that can be applied by anyone:

Tables display data in rows and columns, are easy to create in PowerPoint 2007, and is a great way to represent textual data. When using tables, consider including only the subset of data that's most relevant as well as highlighting key data in a different color or font weight to avoid overwhelming the audience with too much information.

Data charts come in many forms ranging from pie charts to bar graphs, and are frequently used because they are well suited for many types of quantitative data.

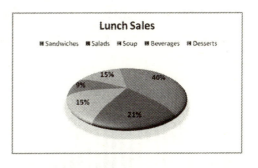

Although it's possible to enter data directly in PowerPoint 2007 to create charts, it's better to create them in Excel (or similar application) and paste them as *Enhanced Metafiles* (not as Excel objects) into a presentation. There are many reasons for this two-step process:

• Frequently data are already in Excel, so there is no need to re-create them in PowerPoint 2007. Fortunately, it's possible to control just about every aspect of chart display (e.g. symbol color, line weight) in Excel, so there's no loss in functionality when creating charts in Excel.

• Excel has additional features such as the PivotTable function that allow you to manipulate data and create corresponding charts not possible in PowerPoint 2007.

• Entering data in a presentation can give unintended access to the raw data (if emailed or distributed electronically) instead of just showing the results.

• Embedding numerous charts can significantly increase a presentation's file size. Although PowerPoint 2007 generates files that are smaller in size than those from previous versions, it's still good practice to reduce file size when possible.

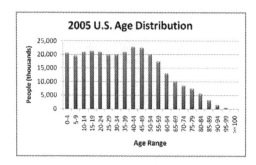

Histograms depict the frequency of occurrence of some measured entity, usually in a column chart form. Histograms are also useful for quantizing otherwise continuous data into discrete data bins, which can be easily created using Excel's built-in function found in the Data Analysis ToolPak Add-In.

Harvey Balls use circular pictograms to indicate the degree to which a particular item meets a criterion. Popularized by Consumer Reports, Harvey Balls are especially useful for visually evaluating many qualitative characteristics at once. While PowerPoint 2007 does not provide Harvey Balls, you can create them as .PNG files and paste into a presentation.

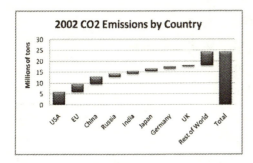

Waterfall charts use floating columns to illustrate changes in values in one dimension as measured against another dimension. This technique is especially useful for visualizing each component's contribution to the whole. Waterfall charts can be constructed in Excel by splitting the data series for a stacked column chart into two series and using the second series to represent cumulative values. Then, turn off the second series' Line and Fill attributes to create a floating appearance for the remaining columns.[8]

---

[8] "Fancy Waterfall Chart." *peltiertech.com*. 9 February 2007. <http://peltiertech.com/Excel/Charts/Waterfall2.html>.

2x2 matrices are commonly used to compare data along two dimensions. Frequently, data also fall into four meaningful quadrants. The Portfolio Matrix, popularized by The Boston Consulting Group, and Gartner's Magic Quadrant, are good examples of 2x2 matrices. 2x2 matrices can be easily constructed by using PowerPoint 2007's table or AutoShapes features.

Portfolio Matrix

Stars | Question Marks

Cash Cows | Dogs

Growth Rate

Market Share

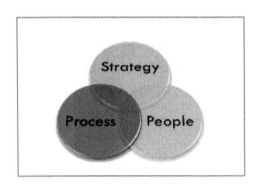

Venn diagrams are typically characterized as overlapping circles that show the logical relationship among groups of things. Venn diagrams are part of PowerPoint 2007's SmartArt suite of charts.

Process flow diagrams depict the sequence of steps of some process, and can be constructed using PowerPoint 2007's AutoShapes

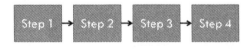

feature. Usually, process diagrams comprise of rectangular boxes, each labeled with the step's name and connected by arrows to the next step.

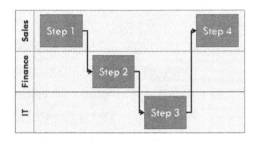

Swim lane diagrams are like process flow diagrams but with the addition of ownership assignment for the steps. Each owner is represented by a swim lane running across the diagram. Corresponding tasks are depicted inside that owner's swim lane.

Pareto charts arose from the Pareto principle, also known as the 80-20 rule, where it is observed 80% of the consequences result from 20% of the causes. Pareto charts

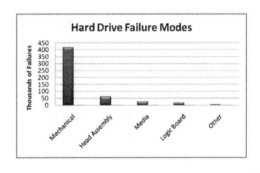

typically display the frequency of occurrence in descending order and the cumulative percentage of the total number of occurrences so that it is easy to see which causes make the greatest contributions to the results.

In addition to the chart types listed above, there are many others also in use. For a general survey, see "A Periodic Table of Visualization Methods" at visual-literacy.org.[9]

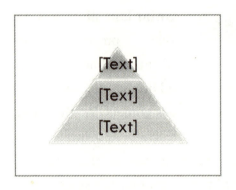

Although some chart types have to be created manually, others can be readily made using PowerPoint 2007's SmartArt feature. SmartArt allows you to choose from a list of built-in charts and diagrams and customize them as desired. Additionally, you can enter text and assign labels directly in SmartArt diagrams. Ironically, the ease of use could actually lessen SmartArt's appeal over time as SmartArt charts become pervasive in presentations, and begin to look like every other SmartArt chart. So, use it sparingly, and consider using SmartArt as a starting point rather than the finish line.

Whether it's an Excel graph, SmartArt chart, or custom diagram, the same UI design guidelines developed for slides also apply:

---

[9] "A Periodic Table of Visualization Methods." *Visual-Literacy.org*. 10 February 2007. <http://www.visual-literacy.org/periodic_table/periodic_table.html>.

- Use the most appropriate data visualization method for the kind of data you have or relationship you want to illustrate.
- Clearly label title, axes (with the correct units of measure), and include a legend if appropriate.
- Use contrasting colors for chart background and data.
- If there will be more than one chart, create them at about the same size.

Make the focus of your chart stand out. This can be accomplished in a number of ways, including: not displaying the entire data set, highlighting specific text or data points, increasing the size of specific text or data points, and turning-off some grid lines while setting the remaining grid lines to light gray or another muted color.

Images

Usually created or edited in specialty graphics software such as Adobe Photoshop, photos and graphics are frequently used in presentations to:

- Highlight or emphasize messages on a slide.
- Depict something that's natively in an image format such as company logo, product picture, etc.
- Convey something more easily done via an image than by text.
- Improve the visual appeal of an otherwise all-text presentation.

 The trick to working with images is having the right photo or graphic so that it complements the rest of the slide naturally instead of looking like being bolted on. Often, images used in a professional environment are custom-made by graphic artists working from storyboards in order to achieve the desired effect. Short of having graphics skills handy, it's not difficult to experiment with stock-art and digital photos to come up with the right image. There are many companies that sell stock-art. It's even possible to find nice photos - like the picture above - in Microsoft's online ClipArt gallery. As you experiment with different images, bear in mind that in general photographic images look more professional than those based on cartoons.

When embedding images, it's best to use the smallest file possible. For example, instead of pasting in a 1MB .JPG digital photo and resize it inside PowerPoint 2007, first compress it in a graphics application such as Microsoft Picture Manager by specifying the approximate dimensions of the image as it would appear on the slide.

Animations & transitions

Animation can significantly enhance the visual impact of a presentation by presenting data or concepts in an engaging manner and providing visual cues to an audience during a live presentation. When done right, animations can add powerfully to the overall audience experience. However, when done poorly, animations can add nothing to a presentation at best, and at worst can make a presentation appear gimmicky and actually confuse the audience. Therefore, knowing when and how best to apply animation is essential. Fortunately, even those who might be inexperienced in animation can still learn to make use of it by following a few simple rules:

- Don't worry about creating animations unless there will be enough time to spend on it (see *STEP 2 Determine Delivery Format & Time Available*).
- If there is sufficient time, evaluate where in the presentation animation can really make a difference - the threshold is obviously subjective but should correspond to a significant improvement to the audience experience, and pick only one or two things on a slide to animate. Too much animation on a slide defeats the purpose of highlighting and emphasizing.
- Presentations made for standalone consumption should avoid animations as readers would be unfamiliar with how the animations are triggered (i.e. mouse-click, timer, event-driven) and would have either wait or keep clicking.

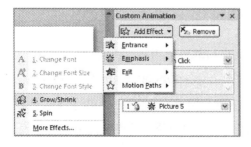

PowerPoint 2007 provides native support for animation for text, object, and chart content. For example, entry and exit events on a slide can be animated. Furthermore, text entry can appear by the letter, by the word, or a paragraph at a time. It's also possible to use animation effects to emphasize a bullet point or a paragraph. Similarly, an object's behavior on a slide can also be animated. When it comes to working with animations developed outside of PowerPoint 2007 such as Flash and Quicktime movies, it's probably better launch them outside of a presentation because PowerPoint 2007 can only link to Flash and Quicktime files. Additionally, since movies frequently need to be played at full screen it might make little sense to embed them inside a presentation anyway.

A note about sound effects. Although it's easy to use sounds in a presentation, it's not trivial to do so seamlessly and effectively. For example, using sound effects (e.g. applause) in conjunction with animation is especially prone to appearing gimmicky. However, there are certain situations, such as playing back a recorded speech to quote someone on an important statement or idea, where sound can strengthen a presentation. Therefore, use sound effects judiciously and sparingly.

As a draft of your presentation emerges, start reading through it from beginning to end to get an overall feel, and pay particular attention to how well the story line and key messages stand out (or don't stand out). At this stage, it's not unusual to have to make edits ranging from rearranging the order of certain slides to making wholesale changes to content. Getting all this right takes some practice, but it's definitely worth doing. For instance, because data visualization appears so often in presentations but is not always trivial to create, learning how to represent information can really make a difference in a presentation. For some inspiration on the subject, check out Edward Tufte's fine works. It would also be valuable to send out the presentation for review.

Finally, even in today's broadband network environment, it's good practice to keep the file size of your presentation small. A large file can result in practical problems for your audience (e.g. emailing a presentation for a conference call but takes too long to open) as well as a perceived annoyance for a long presentation.

STEP 6 Rehearse

Like a theatrical performance, a live presentation is an experienced product. Even with a great story line and dazzling visual effects, any presentation can still bomb with poor storytelling. In fact, it's useful to think not in terms of "making a presentation" but in terms of "giving a performance." All else being equal, a great performance can win over an audience with only a mediocre presentation, but a poor performance can ruin even the best of presentations. Therefore, except for those who are naturally gifted at performing on the fly, it's really important to rehearse. Depending on the situation, it might make sense to actually spend more time on rehearsing for the presentation than on creating it.

As you think about how to verbalize the content of a presentation, keep in mind that you don't want to simply read aloud what's on each slide (some reading is okay for emphasis). Having said that, you do want to refer to each slide's contents - particularly ones with a lot of information - while presenting because otherwise it can be confusing and frustrating for your audience try to reconcile what they see with what they hear. Ideally, you want the slide's content to complement what you have to say, and vice versa. To this end, it might be necessary sketch out your narrative ahead of time. While it's okay to use notes, it's not okay to read from a script. Fortunately, PowerPoint 2007 provides two features that are helpful in this regard.

Presenter's notes

Every PowerPoint 2007 slide has a corresponding notes page, which can be seen in the *Normal View* just below the slide. Notes pages support both text and graphics, and can be used as a working space to develop your narrative. Additionally, because notes page content is not normally projected on the audience's display but can be displayed on the presenter's monitor, you can refer to a slide's notes during your presentation.

Presenter's view

The presenter's view in PowerPoint 2007 can be used to display slides and notes on your monitor at the same time your presentation is displayed on the audience's screen. Presenter's view can be very useful during your 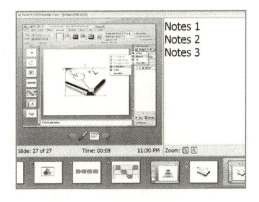 presentation because you can use the presenter's view to look at notes, make annotations, or navigate to another slide. To activate the presenter's view, both displays must be connected to your computer.

With the narrative in place, you can practice your presentation as it would be given in front of an audience. Preferably, you should simulate the actual conditions by rehearsing where the presentation would take place and in the manner it would be presented. In particular, you want to ensure:

- Familiarity with the facilities and audio visual equipment.
- Presentation's total run-time is within the allotted time.
- If using presenter's notes, knowing when and how to refer to them during the presentation.
- Intimacy with the content such that you can tell your story with only minimal reference to presenter's notes.

- A level of comfort with speaking in front of an audience such that it feels like telling a story rather than reading a statement. Examples of expressing this comfort include speaking clearly, making eye contacts, using your arms and hand gestures, and walking amongst the audience.

When it comes to virtual delivery - particularly when you can't see your audience, and vice-versa - your challenge of engaging the audience becomes magnified because usually there is a loss in fidelity (i.e. audience can't see you) and it's easier for your audience to get distracted (e.g. doing something else on their computers). Although this setup is less than ideal from a presenter's point of view, you will almost certainly encounter it in today's globally connected workplace. Fortunately, there are a few things you can do to address these challenges - and even turn them into your advantage:

- Ask remote participants in the same vicinity to gather in a conference room instead of calling in from their individual desks.
- All else being equal, avoid emailing or distributing your presentation in advance. Instead, use an online meeting tool such as WebEx to deliver each page of your presentation synchronized with your narrative in realtime. Doing so prevents the audience from flipping through your presentation ahead of time, which can not only be distracting, but also ruin the potential impact of your narrative. Additionally, online

meeting tools often provide features such as voting and whiteboarding that can add another dimension to the experience.

- If you have friends among the audience, they can use instant messaging to give you live feedback on how things are going and any adjustments you might want to make.

It should come as little surprise that presenting in front of an audience is very much about public speaking and relating to people. Although some people are more naturally gifted at this art than others, one thing everyone can do to improve his or her own ability - regardless of current level - is to practice. Dale Carnegie, known for his public speaking courses and the book "How to Win Friends & Influence People", developed many ideas that are also just as applicable to effective presentations. Many of Mr. Carnegie's lessons[10] have been adapted as they apply to making presentations, and are listed below:

On building rapport

- Smile.
- Remember people's names.
- Begin in a friendly way.
- Become genuinely interested in other people.
- Give honest and sincere appreciation.
- Make the other person feel important - and do it sincerely.

---

[10] Carnegie, Dale. *How to Win Friends & Influence People.* New York: Simon & Schuster, 1998.

On telling your story

- Don't condemn or complain.
- Talk in terms of the other people's interests.
- Arouse in the other person an eager want.
- Appeal to the nobler motives.
- Dramatize your ideas.
- Throw down a challenge.
- Get the other person saying "yes, yes".
- Let the other person feel the idea is his.
- Make the other person happy to do the thing you suggest.

On handling audience questions & feedback

- Be a good listener.
- Avoid an argument.
- Show respect for the other person's opinions. Never say "you're wrong."
- Try honestly to see things from the other person's point of view.
- Be sympathetic with the other person's desires.

Checklist

We've covered quite a bit of territory in a short amount of time. Although there are many considerations in creating an effective presentation, they revolve around a set of simple steps as described previously, and are presented below in a checklist for easy reference.

STEP 1 Define Topic & Goals

✓ Choose subject matter and define scope.

✓ Identify scenario: inform, educate, persuade, sell.

STEP 2 Determine Delivery Format & Time Available

- ✓ Determine delivery format and length of presentation.

- ✓ Survey facilities (if live delivery).

- ✓ Determine available working time and duration.

- ✓ Target presentation fidelity.

STEP 3 Assess Audience Needs

- ✓ Identify key members of audience.

- ✓ Assess audience needs.

STEP 4 Outline & Storyboard

- ✓ Organize ideas into an outline.

- ✓ Write headlines and refine outline.

- ✓ Design storyboard.

STEP 5 Author Content & Refine

- ✓ Design overall look & feel.

- ✓ Create data visualizations (as needed).

- ✓ Create media (as needed).

- ✓ Author content.

- ✓ Refine and iterate.

STEP 6 Rehearse

- ✓ Develop narrative.

- ✓ Familiarize with facilities and presentation equipment.

- ✓ Practice, practice, practice.

Tips & Tricks

Whereas *Checklist* outlines the essential steps in creating effective presentations, this chapter references a set of techniques and best practices that can be selectively applied to your presentations as desired.

Using PowerPoint 2007

Visualizing Data

Influencing & Persuading Your Audience

Putting It All Together: An Example

Now let's take everything we've learned and apply them in an example. Our goal here is not to win a PowerPoint beauty contest (even if there were such a thing), but to demonstrate what's possible by simply following the steps outlined above along with a little bit of work.

In this hypothetical scenario, you have been working on a project at AlphaGRFX (a fictitious company) looking at its

European printer ink business, and will be making a presentation to the management team with your recommendations.[11]

AlphaGRFX overview

AlphaGRFX is a manufacturer of specialized computer and printer equipment for media design firms. Globally headquartered in Boston, Massachusetts, AlphaGRFX sells its products in the United States and Europe through a direct sales force. You recently joined AlphaGRFX's Boston office as a financial analyst and have been working for the past two months at the European headquarters in Amsterdam, Netherlands, analyzing AlphaGRFX's European printer ink business. After looking at the financial data, talking with customers, and working with other departments, you are ready to make a series of recommendations.

STEP1: Choose Topic & Goals

Your topic is what should be done with AlphaGRFX's European printer ink business, which no one at AlphaGRFX fully understands because ink is such a small ticket item with very little attention paid to it. As such, your purpose is two-fold:

---

[11] This example was adapted to demonstrate concepts outlined in the book and is not meant to advocate how to handle a particular business situation. Although certain terminology used could be new to some readers, the underlying concepts should be accessible for most.

- Raise awareness of the importance of the ink business.
- Persuade the audience to adopt and implement a series of recommendations to grow the ink business.

STEP2: Determine Delivery Media & Time Available

You knew at the start of the project that a major deliverable is a live presentation in front of 20 or so people. Additionally, the electronic version of your presentation could also be emailed to others who could not be in attendance. Therefore, even though you didn't know in the beginning exactly what you would ultimately recommend, you could start to think about the kind of story you would like to tell. In fact, this thought process brings clarity to what you should work on and how to go about that work. As a result, you can make the best use of the two weeks at the end of the project to create and rehearse your presentation.

STEP3: Assess Audience Needs

Your audience consists of the project's sponsor - Vice President of the European business unit, managers from various departments including product development, finance, and operations, your supervisor, and peers. As you can see, the makeup of your audience is quite diverse. The variety in job functions means there are likely differences in the audience's backgrounds, interests, and needs. Therefore, you want to be deliberate in choosing which members of the audience to really target and in deciding how to address their needs. In order to make this assessment, it's useful to have a sense for how decisions are made and how things get done at AlphaGRFX (although some readers might think understanding organizational dynamics constitutes "office politics" and want to have nothing to do with it, in practice it is entirely relevant and important because in the end it's about persuading people). Ideally, you should develop this awareness through interactions with people along the way. But even if that doesn't happen, it is possible to still make some good inferences based on typical organizational dynamics as illustrated below.

In terms of targeting certain members of the audience, the Vice President should be at the top of the list because your recommendations would likely affect how she runs her ink business. Next, representatives from other departments are also important because they might have influence with the Vice President or because your recommendations could impact them in some way. Finally, your peers are, generally speaking, a less important constituency because they don't really have any stake in the outcomes. Where does your supervisor fits in all this - after all, shouldn't he be high on the list too? Of course, you want to create a good experience for your supervisor. But with respect to raising his awareness and persuading him, you shouldn't have to do that during the live presentation because he should have already seen and agreed to everything. You see, the Vice President is his boss, and the other managers are his peers. As such, your presentation is in a way his presentation, and it would be a real faux pas for you to present in front of his boss and peers ideas he disagrees with (unless that is your intended outcome). Therefore, in order to avoid such awkward situations, you should review your presentation with your supervisor while it's being developed so that there won't be any surprises. Often, your supervisor can even become your mentor and ally. Not only can he act as a sounding board for your ideas, but he can also provide insights to the needs of your audience and organizational dynamics.

When addressing your targeted audience's needs, it's important to watch out for general considerations described in the preceding chapters (e.g. Cialdini's Six Weapons of Influence) as well as needs unique to this audience. In particular, you have to address:

- Why you are qualified to make any recommendations at all, since you're new to AlphaGRFX and come from a different office.
- What is the ink business and why anyone should care.
- What's the current state of affairs and what's wrong with doing nothing.
- What alternatives have you considered and why are your recommendations the right ones.

• What will it take to adopt your recommendations, how will they work, and what will be the benefits.

STEP 4, 5: Outline & Storyboard, Author Content & Refine

Because steps 4 and 5 are iterative, they are presented together to avoid duplication of content. We will use a modified version of the *Project Summary* template from *STEP 4 Outline & Storyboard*. If possible, go to the actual room and project a test slide to make sure the fonts and colors are readable and look good from where the audience will sit.

STEP 4: Outline & Storyboard

The title slide should display a concise caption of your topic, but should otherwise be uncluttered. While this slide is shown you can make any necessary introductions as well as establish your credibility. Importantly, recognize with whom you've worked on this project (ideally members in the audience) as well as other support and collaboration that took place. Depending on how forcefully you want to make the point, you could even create specific slides for this purpose.

STEP 5: Author Content & Refine

A custom template was used. It has a simple gray on white background that looks clean and professional.

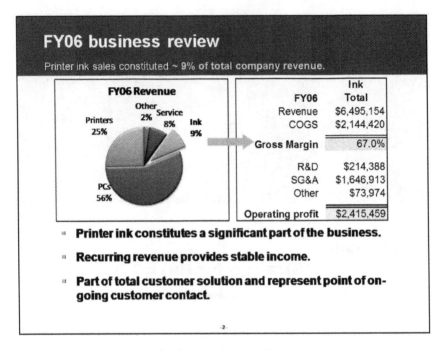

STEP4: Outline & Storyboard

This is the "why anyone should care" slide. By showing that printer ink is ~9% of total revenue and is profitable, you get people's attention. Cite figures in the slide to support your claim in the first bullet point, and strengthen your claim by connecting it to the second and third bullet points.

STEP5: Author Content & Refine

Chart and table were created in Excel 2007 and pasted as *Enhanced Metafile*. Notice the "Ink" slice of the pie chart appears accentuated by being physically separate from the rest of the chart and being labeled. Also notice the arrow pointing from the Ink slice to the table - signifying figures in the table correspond to the Ink business.

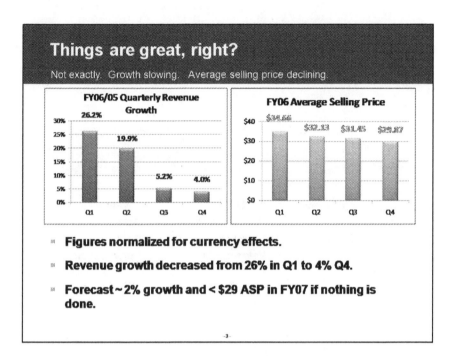

STEP4: Outline & Storyboard

This is the "why should we do anything now" slide. Use trending data to emphasize importance and urgency of the situation. Having established in the previous slide that ink is an important part of the overall business, it's relatively easy to make the point that slowing growth and declining Average Selling Price (ASP) are causes for concern.

STEP5: Author Content & Refine

Charts were created in Excel 2007 and pasted as *Enhanced Metafile*. Additionally, note how a two-line headline can be used to frame the main message of this slide in the form of question and response.

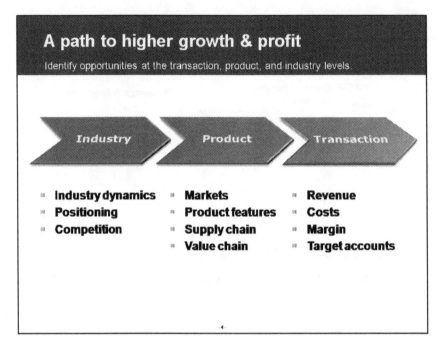

STEP4: Outline & Storyboard

Before diving into details, it's useful to communicate your method of problem analysis and solution synthesis. By doing so, the audience can see that a holistic approach has been used, and can better integrate each piece of new information in context. In this case, you will discuss issues at the industry, product, and transaction levels.

STEP5: Author Content & Refine

The chevron graphic was created using SmartArt.

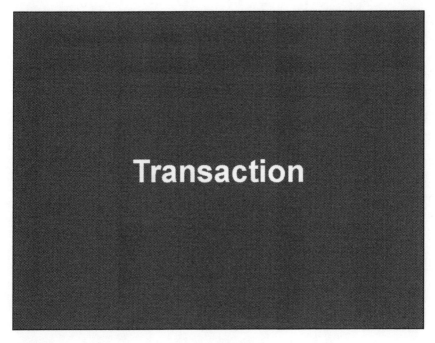

STEP4: Outline & Storyboard
Examining transaction data (i.e. individual ink sales) is a great way to develop a sense for how things are going, and is your starting point.

STEP5: Author Content & Refine
A simple segue content guide was used to introduce the Transaction section. Furthermore, the *Dissolve* slide transition animation was used to reinforce the visual cue of topic transition.

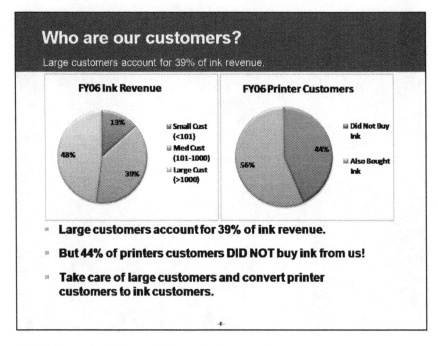

STEP4: Outline & Storyboard

Analysis of transactions effects begins with an understanding of customers. Sales data show while large customers are important, equally important are printer customers who don't currently buy ink from AlphaGRFX.

STEP5: Author Content & Refine

Data was first manipulated in Excel 2007, whose resultant charts were pasted as *Enhanced Metafiles*.

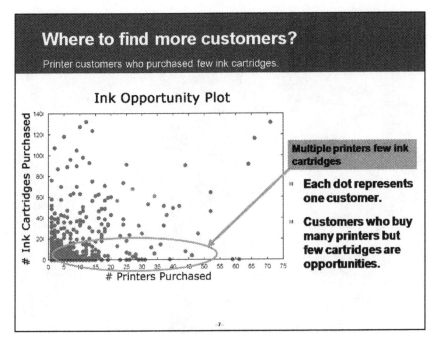

STEP4: Outline & Storyboard

Further analysis of the relationship between printer purchase and ink sales reveals there is a straightforward opportunity with customers who buy many printers but few ink cartridges. Make the point there are simple things that can be done to grow sales. Frequently, the audience expects "low hanging fruit" options.

STEP5: Author Content & Refine

Excel 2007 doesn't create plots, so the plot above was generated using a 3rd party plotting software with data from Excel. The plot was saved as a .PNG file and imported into PowerPoint 2007.

STEP4: Outline & Storyboard

After identifying specific opportunities at the transaction level, segue to the industry level.

STEP5: Author Content & Refine

Again, a content guide slide with *Dissolve* animation was used to introduce the next topic.

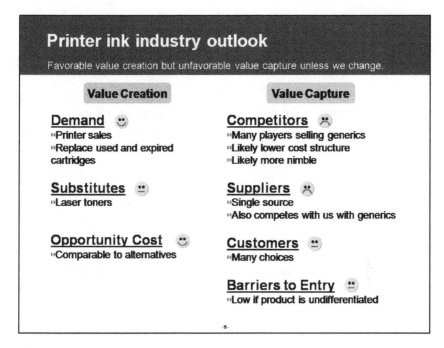

STEP4: Outline & Storyboard

As an industry, there is a lot of money to be made in printer ink business (value creation). However, for a number of reasons, AlphaGRFX is not well positioned to extract value for itself (value capture).

STEP5: Author Content & Refine

This slide has a lot of text. One way to help your audience grasp the main points without having to read every word is by using something like smiley icons. They were created using a 3rd party web graphics package and imported as .PNG files. Each smiley icon was animated with the *Blinds* animation and would be displayed as each bullet point is discussed.

Is it a good industry?

Yes, it can be.

"Our margins for ink continue to remain generally higher than our margins for printers. We hope to sell more ink cartridges in the future as more customers recognize the benefits of our ink, which perform better than those of the generic substitutes."
Competitor A, 2005 10-K filing with SEC

"Our business strategy is centered on rapidly building an installed base of printers in order to maximize the potential recurring revenue associated from sales of our disposable ink cartridges."
Competitor B, 2004 10-K filing with SEC

-10-

STEP4: Outline & Storyboard

Is it possible that nobody makes any money? Although there are some industries in that category (satellite radio being one), it appears AlphaGRFX's competitors are doing just fine.

STEP5: Author Content & Refine

Usually, making your audience read every word on a slide is not a good idea, but here is a case where that's exactly what we want. When trying to make the point that AlphaGRFX's problems are unique, quoting competitors from their annual reports can be especially effective. Excerpts were selected from the US Securities Exchange Commission's website at http://www.sec.gov. *Color Typewriter* animation was used to cue the audience to read along by displaying one word at a time.

Our positioning

We're the industry's premier provider.

NuTEC is the #1 provider of computing solutions for the new media industry, and earns a premium by delivering differentiated products and services.

However...

We frequently end up competing on price on printer ink, resulting in lost sales and declining average selling price.

-11-

STEP4: Outline & Storyboard

A probable reason why AlphaGRFX is doing worse than its competitors is although AlphaGRFX usually commands a premium for its other products, it unwittingly ends up competing on price in its ink business and thereby destroying profits.

STEP5: Author Content & Refine

Clearly make the distinction between AlphaGRFX's positioning and what's actually happening by separating the two descriptions and using a different color to highlight the contrast.

So, what should we do?

Do what is consistent with our positioning and strengths.

Use printer installed base to grow recurring revenue **from ink at** higher margins.

by targeting the following in FY07

- **Grow revenue by +20%.**

- **Maintain current account-level margins.**

- **Increase ink cartridge market share of exiting printer customers from 56% to 60%.**

-12-

STEP4: Outline & Storyboard

Reconcile the inconsistency between AlphaGRFX's positioning and reality by advocating for refocusing on being a premium vendor and using printer sales to grow ink sales more profitably. Additionally, set specific and measurable targets.

STEP5: Author Content & Refine

Colors were used to highlight key words.

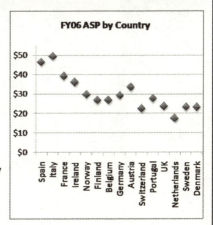

STEP4: Outline & Storyboard

Someone in the audience might think lowering price will lead to more sales, but this would almost certainly be a bad idea. Pre-empt this question by showing why lowering price does not make sense.

STEP5: Author Content & Refine

Chart was created in Excel 2007 and pasted as *Enhanced Metafile.*

STEP4: Outline & Storyboard
Next, segue to topics at the product level.

STEP5: Author Content & Refine
Again, a content guide slide with *Dissolve* animation was used to introduce the next topic.

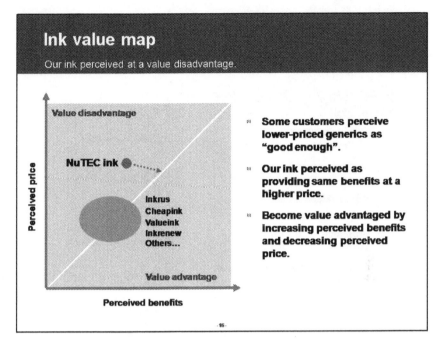

STEP4: Outline & Storyboard

One way to think about whether AlphaGRFX has the right ink product is to compare it with competitor's products with respect to features and price for the customer. Although customers prefer AlphaGRFX's brand, they also perceive AlphaGRFX's ink product as delivering roughly the same amount of benefits as those from generic manufacturers but at a higher price. Therefore, AlphaGRFX should look to improve its ink product so that it becomes a better deal for customers.

STEP5: Author Content & Refine

Custom chart was created by combining stock shapes in PowerPoint 2007.

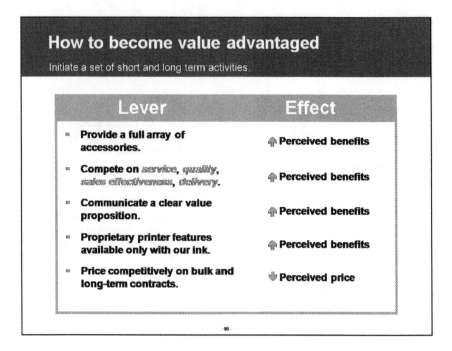

STEP4: Outline & Storyboard

AlphaGRFX can enhance customer's perception of bang for the buck by taking a number of steps that together can increase perceived benefits and decrease perceived price of its ink.

STEP5: Author Content & Refine

Colors were used to emphasize key ideas. Additionally, arrows were used to represent increase/decrease.

STEP4: Outline & Storyboard

Finally, tie all of the ideas discussed previously into a holistic plan.

STEP5: Author Content & Refine

Again, a content guide slide with *Dissolve* animation was used to introduce the next topic.

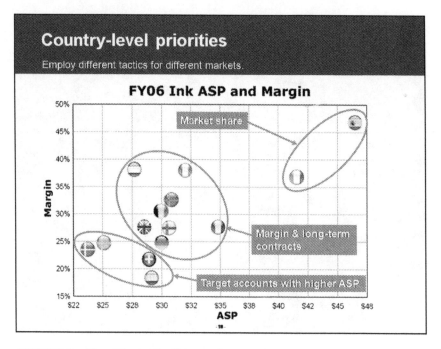

STEP4: Outline & Storyboard

Although each country operates in an unique business environment, multiple countries can be grouped together for planning purposes. For example, countries still holding on to high ASP and margin should expand market share, while countries with low ASP and margin should target customers with high ASP.

STEP5: Author Content & Refine

Rather than listing countries by name, it's easier to get an overall sense of your recommendations by representing countries with icons. Icons and chart were created using 3rd party applications, imported into PowerPoint 2007, and then annotated.

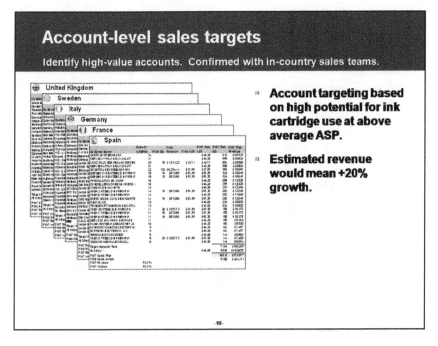

STEP4: Outline & Storyboard

Based on the tactics outlined previously, identify targeted customers and associated sales goals for each country.

STEP5: Author Content & Refine

A number of plans, each with a list of targeted customers, can be used to convey the message that your proposal is not just a high level blueprint, but is also a detailed operations plan. Each plan corresponds to an Excel file and was pasted in the slide as *Enhanced Metafile*.

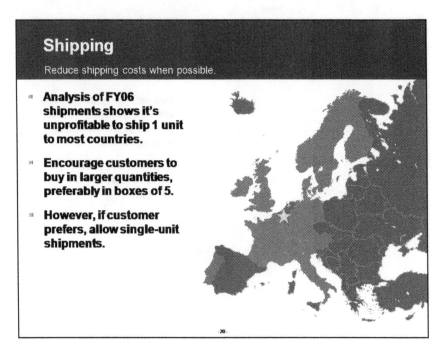

STEP4: Outline & Storyboard

Data analysis shows AlphaGRFX actually loses money when shipping single ink cartridges to countries in pink. Therefore, profit margins can be improved by selling and shipping in bulk when possible.

STEP5: Author Content & Refine

Two sets of graphics were used. One set represents a background map of Europe (in purple). The other set represents a graphic for each country (in pink) where AlphaGRFX loses money when shipping single units. When the slide is initially displayed, only the background map of Europe is shown. Then, the *Entrance* animation displayed each country's graphic sequentially.

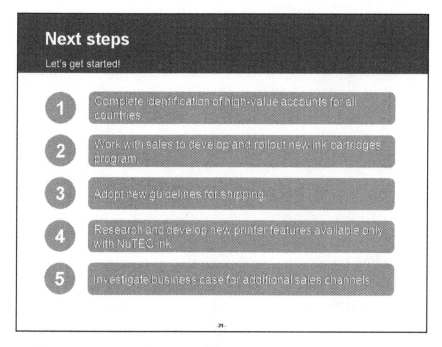

STEP4: Outline & Storyboard

Finally, summarize recommendations in terms of next steps.

STEP5: Author Content & Refine

Stock shapes in PowerPoint 2007 were used to create an enhanced bulleted list to draw the audience's attention. The *Entrance* animation was applied to display one bullet point at a time.

STEP 6: Rehearse

Now that we have created a complete presentation, it's time to focus on topics involved in delivering the presentation in front of your audience.

First, you can add a narrative that will, along with the slides, communicate your story and highlight its key messages. In summary, your audience should hear something like:

1. You have been collaborating with various groups over the past two months to analyze AlphaGRFX's European printer ink business, and have important findings to share.

2. Printer ink constitutes an important part of the overall AlphaGRFX business, and contributed 9% to total revenue in fiscal year 2006.

3. However, the outlook is gloomy - evidenced by declining growth and ASP, and requires action.

4. In order to determine the best course of action in a comprehensive and holistic manner, analyses were performed at the transaction, product, and industry levels.

5. At the transaction level, data show while large customers contribute a significant portion to total ink revenue, many printer customers are not buying ink from AlphaGRFX, and represent an area of great opportunity.

6. It's possible to identify which customers could be targeted by looking at purchase history of printer and ink purchases.

7. At the industry level, though the printer ink business can be very lucrative, AlphaGRFX is not well positioned to successfully capture significant potential industry earnings.

8. Although one might wonder whether the ink business is good for anybody, evidence from direct competitors suggests they are doing quite well.

9. A root cause of AlphaGRFX's current dilemma is selling its ink as a commodity and ending up competing solely on price. Instead, AlphaGRFX should play to its strengths and use its printer installed base to sell ink with a focus on higher margins. Even conservative estimates could reverse the decline in growth and improve margins.

10. Although some might still argue lowering price can also re-energize sales, numerous reasons argue this is a choice of last resort.

11. At the product level, customers perceive AlphaGRFX as overpriced for the functionalities provided. Therefore, AlphaGRFX should seek to improve the customer's perception of "bang for the buck." Specifically, there are a number of R&D, marketing, and sales activities that can increase perceived value and decrease perceived price.

12. In terms of overall strategy, AlphaGRFX should

- consider each country's ink business as contributing to a larger whole and part of an integrated strategy.
- countries that still have relatively high ASP and margin should focus on increasing market share.
- countries that are already under pricing pressure should focus on customers who can generate higher margins.

13. Account-level sales plans were developed based on the strategy above, and is in process of being rolled out to sales teams.

14. Another way to improve margins is to reduce costs. AlphaGRFX should encourage customers to purchase more than one ink cartridge at a time to reduce shipping costs.

15. In summary, AlphaGRFX should:

- complete identification of high-value accounts for all countries.

- work with sales to develop and rollout new ink cartridges program.

- adopt new guidelines for shipping.

- research and develop new printer features available only with AlphaGRFX ink.

- investigate additional sales channels such as selling through retailers.

Next, checkout the facilities in which the live presentation will take place. If possible, rehearse your presentation in this room as the more comfortable you become with the physical environment, the more you will feel at ease during your presentation. Pay particular attention to the topics discussed previously:

- Familiarity with the facilities and audio visual equipment.
- Presentation's total run-time is within the allotted time.
- If using presenter's notes, knowing when and how to refer to them during the presentation.

- Intimacy with the content such that you can tell your story with only minimal reference to slides or presenter's notes.
- A level of comfort with speaking in front of an audience.

Finally, practice, practice, and practice!

Final Thoughts

Over the preceding chapters, we saw why it's important to be able to tell a compelling story, and developed a holistic approach that makes achieving this goal straightforward for and accessible to beginners. My hope is that with some simple tools, even those with little experience can create effective and winning presentations. Of course, the principles discussed here are not meant to be letters-of-law, but rather as rules-of-thumb. With some practice and experience, it should become easier and more natural to apply only those guidelines that make sense for you while developing your own personal style. In the end, technological advances and an abundance of available presentation software notwithstanding, storytelling is still an uniquely human craft and ultimately rests on your ability to communicate in a way that makes the story come alive. So, what's *your* story?

www.ingramcontent.com/pod-product-compliance
Lightning Source LLC
Chambersburg PA
CBHW051252050326
40689CB00007B/1167